Foreword: Unlocking the Power of AI

The world we live in today is one of constant change, fueled by technological advancements that are reshaping the way we work, live, and interact. At the heart of this transformation lies artificial intelligence (AI)—a revolutionary force that has moved beyond science fiction to become an integral part of our everyday lives. From smartphones that predict our typing to chatbots that answer our questions, AI is no longer a tool of the future—it is here, and it is changing the game.

When I first encountered AI, I was both fascinated and skeptical. The potential seemed limitless, but the complexity was daunting. It felt like a realm reserved for tech experts and engineers. But as I began to explore its applications, I realized something profound: AI is not just for the tech-savvy elite—it is a tool for everyone. Whether you're an entrepreneur striving to scale your business, a professional seeking to optimize workflows, or a creative looking for inspiration, AI offers opportunities to unlock new levels of productivity and efficiency.

This book is born from that realization. My goal is not to overwhelm you with technical jargon or complex theories but to empower you with practical insights and actionable strategies. AI is not about replacing humans—it's about augmenting our abilities, enabling us to do more with less effort, and allowing us to focus on what truly matters.

As you journey through this book, you'll discover the transformative power of AI and how it can revolutionize the way you work. Together, we'll explore the tools, techniques, and trends that are shaping the AI landscape. Whether you're a beginner just stepping into the world of AI or someone already familiar with its potential, this book is designed to guide you, inspire you, and help you harness the incredible power of AI to achieve your goals.

The time to embrace AI is now. It's not just a buzzword or a passing trend—it's a key to unlocking a smarter, more efficient future. Let this book be your guide as we take the first step into that future together.

Let's dive in and unlock the possibilities.

- Luke

Introduction

You know, if someone told me a few years ago that artificial intelligence (AI) would become the secret weapon for getting more done in less time, I would've probably laughed and said, "Sure, sounds like something out of a sci-fi movie." But here we are—AI isn't just some futuristic concept anymore. It's real, it's here, and it's changing the way we work every single day. And guess what? It's not just for tech geniuses or mega-corporations anymore. You and I? We can use it too. Actually, we *should* use it.

Let me paint a picture for you: imagine waking up in the morning and knowing that your email is already sorted, your schedule is perfectly optimized, and the first draft of that daunting report you've been procrastinating on is ready. All while you slept. Sounds pretty amazing, right? That's the power of AI when you know how to use it. It's not about replacing you (no robot is coming for your job—at least not yet); it's about making your work easier, smarter, and yes, a little more enjoyable.

Why AI is a Game-Changer for Productivity

Let's be real—work has gotten more demanding than ever. Deadlines seem tighter, to-do lists are never-ending, and the pressure to keep up with everything can feel overwhelming. It's like we're constantly trying to swim upstream while carrying a bag of bricks. But what if I told you AI can take that bag, lighten the load, and even help you glide through the current?

Here's what makes AI so special: it takes repetitive, time-consuming tasks off your plate, letting you focus on the things that really matter. You know, the stuff that requires creativity, decision-making, and actual human connection. Whether it's drafting an email, analyzing data, or even scheduling meetings, AI can handle the grunt work, and it does it faster and more accurately than we ever could. Think of it like having the ultimate assistant who never sleeps, never complains, and works 24/7.

But here's the thing—you don't need to be some kind of tech wizard to make this work for you. With the right tools and a bit of guidance, you can integrate AI into your daily life, no matter what your job is or how "non-techy" you think you are. I've been there myself. When I first started exploring AI, it felt a little intimidating. But as I began experimenting and learning, I realized that these tools are designed to be accessible, even for people like me who once thought "automation" was just a fancy buzzword. And trust me, if I can figure this out, you can too.

What This Book Will Do for You

This book is your guide to making AI your productivity superpower. I've broken everything down into simple, actionable steps that anyone can follow, whether you're an absolute beginner or someone who's already dipped their toes into the AI world. My goal is to help you understand not just *what* AI can do, but *how* to make it work for you—without the fluff, without the jargon, and without wasting hours on trial and error.

Here's what you'll get:

- **Practical tips:** We're talking real-world, no-nonsense advice on how to use AI tools to get more done in less time.
- **Step-by-step guidance:** Whether it's automating tasks, creating content, or organizing your day, I'll show you exactly how to do it. No guesswork.
- **Relatable stories:** I'll share my own experiences (including a few embarrassing mistakes) to make sure you know you're not alone in figuring this out.
- **AI for everyone:** This isn't just for tech professionals. If you're a freelancer, small business owner, corporate employee, or just someone who wants to work smarter, this book is for you.

Who This Book Is For

Now, you might be wondering, "Is this really for me?" Well, let's see:

- Are you a **beginner** who's curious about AI but feels completely lost on where to start?

- Are you a **professional** juggling deadlines, meetings, and emails, wondering if there's a better way to manage it all?
- Are you a **freelancer** or **entrepreneur** trying to grow your business without working 24/7?
- Or maybe you're just someone who wants to reclaim a little more of your time and sanity while still getting things done?

If you nodded your head at any of those, then yes, this book is absolutely for you. I'm here to show you that you don't need to spend weeks or months trying to figure out AI tools on your own. With this guide, you'll learn how to make AI your ally in no time.

Why This Matters Now

Here's the deal—AI isn't going anywhere. In fact, it's evolving faster than ever. Companies are using it. Competitors are using it. And if you don't start using it too, you risk falling behind. But the good news? You don't need to be an early adopter or a tech expert to take advantage of it. You just need the right guidance—and that's what I'm here to provide.

So, grab your coffee, settle in, and get ready to transform the way you work. Whether you're here to save time, boost productivity, or just stay ahead of the curve, I promise this journey will be worth it. Let's dive in together and see what AI can do for *you*.

Understanding AI and Its Potential

Chapter 1: What Is Artificial Intelligence?

Alright, before we jump into the exciting stuff about how artificial intelligence (AI) can completely change the way you work, let's start with the basics. I know, I know—you've probably heard the term "AI" thrown around a million times. It's in the news, it's on your social media feed, and even that annoying chatbot on your favorite shopping site claims to be powered by it. But what exactly is AI? And more importantly, why should you care? Let me break it down for you in the simplest way possible.

What Is Artificial Intelligence?

At its core, artificial intelligence is a fancy way of saying "machines that can think and learn like humans—kind of." AI refers to the technology that enables computers and software to perform tasks that would normally require human intelligence. These tasks can include things like recognizing patterns, understanding natural language (you know, like when Siri magically knows what you mean when you mumble a half-baked question), making decisions, and even solving problems.

But here's the thing: AI doesn't actually "think" the way you and I do. It's not sitting there, contemplating the meaning of life or deciding which flavor of ice cream it wants. It works by using algorithms—basically, a set of instructions—to process massive amounts of data and produce results. It's all about patterns, probabilities, and predictions. Think of it like a really smart assistant who's great at crunching numbers and spotting trends but has zero emotional baggage or bad days.

A Quick (and Painless) History Lesson

Let me give you the crash course on where AI comes from—don't worry, I'll keep it brief. The idea of creating machines that can "think" has been around for centuries. (Ever heard of the myth of the golem? Yeah, people have been into this concept for a *long* time.) But AI as we know it started to take shape in the mid-20th century. Here's the timeline in a nutshell:

- **1950s**: Computer scientist Alan Turing (you've probably heard of him) asked the question: "Can machines think?" He even created the famous Turing Test to measure whether a machine's behavior could pass as human-like.
- **1970s-80s**: AI research had its ups and downs. It was mostly academic and often over-promised (hello, flying cars!), leading to what they called an "AI winter" when funding dried up.

- **1990s-2000s**: Things started picking up again, thanks to faster computers and more data. Remember when IBM's Deep Blue beat the world chess champion? That was a big moment.
- **2010s and beyond**: AI exploded. With the rise of machine learning (where AI learns from data) and deep learning (a more advanced form of machine learning), AI went from theory to reality. Now, it's in your phone, your car, your Netflix recommendations, and even your favorite AI writing assistant. (Ahem, like me.)

The bottom line? AI went from being a sci-fi dream to something we use every day—often without even realizing it.

How Does AI Show Up in Your Work Life?

So, how is AI actually useful for *you*? Let's skip the technical mumbo jumbo and get to the good stuff: the real-life applications. AI is already everywhere in the workplace, helping people work faster, smarter, and, honestly, with less stress. Here are just a few examples:

1. **Voice Assistants**
   Whether you're asking Alexa to remind you about that meeting or getting Google Assistant to send an email hands-free, voice AI tools save you time and effort. Think of them as your always-on helper that doesn't even need coffee breaks.

2. **Content Creation**
   AI can now write blog posts, create social media captions, and even help brainstorm ideas. Tools like Jasper, ChatGPT (hi!), and others are revolutionizing how people create content. You don't need to stare at a blank screen anymore—AI's got your back.
3. **Data Analysis**
   Remember when you used to spend hours sifting through spreadsheets trying to find patterns? AI can do that in seconds. Tools like Power BI or Tableau use AI to visualize data and give you actionable insights. No more squinting at rows and rows of numbers.
4. **Task Automation**
   Repetitive tasks like scheduling meetings, sending follow-ups, or managing invoices? AI can take those off your plate entirely. Platforms like Zapier connect your apps and automate the stuff you'd rather not do.
5. **Customer Support**
   Ever chatted with a customer support bot at 2 a.m.? That's AI at work. While it might not always get it right (we've all been frustrated by one of those bots), it's constantly improving and helping businesses stay available around the clock.
6. **Creative Fields**
   AI isn't just for number-crunchers. Artists, designers, and marketers are using AI tools like Canva or DALL·E to create visuals and designs in record time.

The point is, AI isn't just some nerdy tech thing—it's a productivity tool that's sneaking into pretty much every corner of the modern workplace.

Debunking the Myths: AI Isn't Magic (Or a Monster)

Now, I need to address something: AI gets a bad rap sometimes. Some people think it's this magical, all-knowing thing that's going to take over the world. Others think it's a cold, heartless machine coming for their jobs. Neither of these is true. Let's clear the air.

- **Myth #1: AI is Magic**
  AI is smart, but it's not magic. It doesn't know what you're thinking (thankfully), and it can only do what it's programmed to do. If you ask it to write a report, it's not coming up with earth-shattering ideas—it's using patterns in the data it's been trained on. It's a tool, not a crystal ball.
- **Myth #2: AI Will Replace You**
  AI isn't here to steal your job. It's here to make your job easier. Think of it as a coworker who's great at the boring, repetitive stuff. It can handle the grunt work while you focus on the things that *really* need a human touch—like creativity, strategy, and building relationships.
- **Myth #3: AI Is Only for Tech Experts**
  If you're thinking, "This sounds cool, but I'm not a tech person," I hear you. But trust me, you don't

need to know how to code to use AI tools. They're designed to be user-friendly, and in this book, I'll show you exactly how to make them work for you—no tech degree required.

Why You Should Care

Here's the deal: AI isn't going anywhere. It's only going to get better, faster, and more accessible. Whether you're excited about it or a little skeptical, learning how to use AI is one of the smartest moves you can make right now. It's like learning to drive when cars first became a thing—you don't want to be left behind while everyone else is zipping down the road.

So, let's dive in and figure out how you can make AI work for you—no jargon, no fluff, just practical tips and tools that'll save you time, boost your productivity, and maybe even make work a little more fun. Trust me, it's easier than you think.

Chapter 2: Types of AI Tools

By now, you might be wondering, "Okay, AI sounds cool, but what exactly are these tools? And how do I figure out which ones I actually need?" Don't worry—I've got you covered. In this chapter, we're diving into the different types of AI tools out there, and trust me, it's not as overwhelming as it sounds. Think of it like walking into a hardware store: each tool is designed for a specific purpose. You just need to know which one solves your problem. Let's break it down.

Language Generation Tools: The Ultimate Wordsmiths

You know those times when you're staring at a blank screen, trying to find the perfect way to phrase something? Whether it's an email, a blog post, or even a catchy social media caption, language generation tools are here to save you. These tools are basically like having a writing assistant in your pocket.

Examples:

- **ChatGPT**: I mean, you're reading this, so you've already met me. I can help you brainstorm ideas, draft content, or even create an entire first draft.
- **Jasper**: Another powerhouse tool that specializes in creating marketing copy, blog posts, and other written content. It's perfect for businesses looking to streamline their content creation process.

What They're Good For:

- Writing professional emails (you know, the ones where you don't want to sound like you're yelling "Hey!!!").
- Generating creative ideas when your brain feels like a potato.

- Crafting SEO-friendly blog posts and marketing copy.
- Even writing scripts or speeches when you need some inspiration.

Pro Tip: If writing feels like a chore, or you just don't have time to polish every word, these tools are a game-changer. Just remember, they're not perfect. Always review and tweak the output to make sure it sounds like *you*.

Automation Tools: The Task Masters

Okay, let's talk about those small, repetitive tasks that eat up your day—scheduling meetings, sending follow-up emails, updating spreadsheets. Sound familiar? Automation tools step in to handle all that boring stuff so you can focus on the work that actually matters. It's like having a personal assistant, but without the extra office chair.

Examples:

- **Zapier**: Think of it as the glue that connects your favorite apps. Want to automatically save email attachments to Google Drive? Done. Need to add new leads from a web form into your CRM? Zapier's got it.
- **Automate.io**: Similar to Zapier, but with a simpler interface and some unique integrations. It's perfect for small businesses or solopreneurs.

What They're Good For:

- Automating workflows between apps (e.g., sending Slack notifications when you get a new email).
- Setting up reminders or follow-up emails automatically.
- Syncing data between platforms, so you're not copying and pasting like it's 1999.

Pro Tip: Start small. Pick one or two tasks that you do over and over again, and set up an automation. You'll be amazed at how much time you'll save.

Data Analysis Tools: Your Numbers Guru

Let's face it: most of us aren't exactly thrilled to spend hours digging through spreadsheets. But data is everywhere, and making sense of it can give you a serious edge. That's where AI-powered data analysis tools come in. They don't just crunch the numbers—they turn them into insights you can actually use.

Examples:

- **Power BI**: A Microsoft tool that helps you create stunning visual reports from your data. It's like Excel on steroids.
- **Tableau**: Another big player in the data visualization world. It's incredibly user-friendly and great for

creating dashboards that make your data look like art.

What They're Good For:

- Identifying trends in sales, customer behavior, or website traffic.
- Creating visually appealing reports that make you look like a data wizard in meetings.
- Making better decisions by turning raw data into actionable insights.

Pro Tip: If numbers aren't your thing, don't worry—these tools do most of the heavy lifting. Start with pre-built templates to get a feel for how they work.

Creative Tools: The Artists and Designers

Not all of us are born with a designer's eye or a natural flair for creativity. But that's okay, because AI has our backs here too. Creative tools make it easier than ever to whip up visuals, designs, and even videos, no matter your skill level.

Examples:

- **Canva**: You've probably heard of this one. Canva is a drag-and-drop design tool that now uses AI to suggest layouts, create text-to-image designs, and more.

- **DALL·E**: Feeling extra creative? DALL·E generates stunning, unique images based on text prompts. Want a picture of a "cat in a business suit"? Done.

What They're Good For:

- Creating professional-looking social media graphics, presentations, or marketing materials.
- Generating unique visual content for blog posts, ads, or websites.
- Experimenting with creative ideas without spending hours in Photoshop.

Pro Tip: These tools are perfect for non-designers, but don't be afraid to play around. The more you experiment, the better your results will be.

How to Choose the Right Tool for You

Now that you know the major categories, let's talk about the million-dollar question: How do you pick the right tool? It's easier than you think—just follow these steps:

1. **Identify Your Problem:** What's the one task that eats up your time or stresses you out the most? Start there. For example, if writing is your pain point, try a language generation tool. If data gives you a headache, look into data analysis tools.
2. **Think About Your Workflow:** Look at the tools you already use. Do you live in Gmail? Use Slack every

day? Choose AI tools that integrate seamlessly with your existing apps.

3. **Start Small:** Don't try to overhaul your entire workflow overnight. Pick one or two tools to test out. For instance, you could set up a simple automation with Zapier or use ChatGPT to draft your next email.
4. **Test and Adjust:** Most AI tools have free trials or free versions, so play around and see what works for you. And don't be afraid to tweak the settings or prompts to get the best results.

Why This Matters

Here's the thing: the right AI tool can completely change how you work, but only if you choose one that fits your needs. Don't fall for the hype or feel pressured to use something just because it's trendy. At the end of the day, AI tools are just that—*tools*. They're here to help you save time, reduce stress, and work smarter. And when you find the right ones, it's like having a secret weapon in your productivity arsenal.

So, take a deep breath, pick one or two tools to try, and start experimenting. You've got this!

Chapter 3: Why AI Boosts Productivity

Let me ask you something: how many hours of your day are spent on mind-numbing, repetitive tasks? You know, the stuff like sorting emails, updating spreadsheets, or scheduling meetings. It's not exactly the kind of work that gets you out of bed in the morning, right? If you're like me, these little tasks can pile up and leave you feeling like you're busy all day but not actually getting much done.

That's where AI comes in. It's not just a tool—it's like having an extra pair of hands (or ten) to help you get things done faster, smarter, and with way less stress. Let's break it down and see why AI isn't just helpful—it's a productivity game-changer.

---

1. AI Saves You Time by Handling Data at Lightning Speed

Here's a quick reality check: humans are pretty terrible at processing huge amounts of data. Sure, we can do it, but it takes forever, and let's be honest, mistakes happen. AI, on the other hand, thrives on data. It can process, organize, and analyze massive amounts of information in seconds—things that would take us hours or even days.

Let me give you a real-world example. Picture this: you're working on a report, and you've got to sift through hundreds of survey responses to find trends. Normally, that means scrolling through rows and rows of data until your eyes glaze over. But with AI-powered tools like Power BI or Tableau, you can upload that data, and bam—within minutes, you've got visualized insights that actually make sense.

Or think about customer data. If you're running a small business, you probably have tons of info—emails, purchase history, feedback—that can help you understand your customers better. AI tools can quickly sort through all that, identify patterns, and even make recommendations. Instead of spending hours trying to figure it out yourself, you get actionable insights handed to you on a silver platter.

And let's not forget search functions. Ever spent way too long trying to find *that one file* you know you saved somewhere? AI-powered search (like Google Drive's built-in AI) can locate it for you in seconds, even if you don't remember the exact file name.

Why this matters: Time is your most valuable resource, and AI gives you back hours—hours you can spend on the tasks that really move the needle.

---

2. AI Reduces Repetitive Work and Frees You Up for High-Value Tasks

Let's talk about the soul-sucking chores we all face at work. You know, the ones that feel like they take forever but don't actually require much brainpower. For me, it's things like sending reminder emails, logging data into spreadsheets, and creating endless variations of the same presentation. Sure, they're necessary, but they don't exactly make me feel accomplished.

Here's the good news: AI lives for this kind of work.

- **Automated Emails:** With tools like Zapier, you can set up triggers to send automated emails based on certain actions. Got a new lead? Zapier can instantly send a follow-up email without you lifting a finger.
- **Data Entry:** Instead of manually copying and pasting information between systems, AI can sync everything for you. Tools like Automate.io can connect your apps so data flows seamlessly.
- **Scheduling:** Hate the back-and-forth of scheduling meetings? AI scheduling tools like Calendly can handle it for you, finding times that work for everyone without the endless email chains.

The beauty of AI is that it takes these low-value tasks off your plate so you can focus on the stuff that actually matters—like brainstorming ideas, building strategies, or connecting with clients.

Let me share a personal story. A while back, I was spending hours every week managing a newsletter. Formatting, finding images, writing copy—it was exhausting. Then I started using an AI tool that automated most of it: it pulled content suggestions, created layouts, and even scheduled the emails. Suddenly, what used to take me half a day was done in under an hour.

Why this matters: Your time and energy should go toward things only *you* can do. AI handles the rest, so you're not bogged down by busywork.

---

3. AI Streamlines and Automates Workflows

Here's where things get really cool. AI doesn't just help you with individual tasks—it can connect the dots between them to create an entire workflow that runs almost on autopilot. Imagine your workday running like a well-oiled machine, where every tool and task is synced perfectly. Sounds like a dream, right? Well, with AI, it's not just possible—it's practical.

Let me paint you a picture:

- You use a form on your website to collect customer inquiries.
- Every new submission automatically gets sent to your CRM (customer relationship management) system.
- The system flags high-priority leads based on keywords in their inquiry.
- An AI assistant drafts a personalized response email and schedules a follow-up reminder for you.

All of this happens without you lifting a finger. What used to involve manually downloading data, sorting through emails, and setting up reminders now happens in the background while you focus on other things.

And automation isn't just for big companies with big budgets. Tools like Zapier, IFTTT, and Automate.io make it accessible for everyone. Even if you're running a one-person business, you can create workflows that save you hours every week.

Why this matters: Automation doesn't just save time—it reduces the chances of human error, ensures consistency, and makes your entire workflow smarter.

Why This Is a Game-Changer

Here's the bottom line: AI doesn't just make your work easier—it makes it *better*. By saving time, reducing busywork, and automating workflows, it frees you up to focus on what truly matters. It's not about working harder; it's about working smarter.

Think of it this way: AI is like having a team of highly efficient assistants who can handle the repetitive, data-heavy tasks for you. But instead of hiring a whole new team, you're just using the right tools.

If you're someone who's constantly wishing for more hours in the day, AI isn't just helpful—it's essential. And the best part? You don't need to be an expert to start using it. Even small steps—like automating one repetitive task or using AI to analyze data—can have a massive impact on your productivity.

In the next chapter, we'll start exploring exactly *how* you can incorporate AI into your workday. Trust me, it's easier than you think, and the results will speak for themselves. Ready? Let's keep going.

Getting Started with AI Tools

Chapter 4: Getting Started with ChatGPT and Similar Tools

If there's one AI tool that's been making waves lately, it's ChatGPT. I mean, let's be real—you're reading this book, so you already know how handy it can be. But if you've only scratched the surface of what it can do, you're in for a treat. ChatGPT (and similar tools) isn't just another shiny tech gadget—it's like having a personal assistant, a brainstorming buddy, and a writing coach all rolled into one.

Let me walk you through what it is, how to use it, and most importantly, how to get the best results from it. Trust me, once you see what it can do, you'll wonder how you ever got by without it.

What Is ChatGPT, and What Can It Do?

First, let's get the basics out of the way. ChatGPT is an AI-powered language model that can generate human-like text based on the prompts you give it. That's a fancy way of saying, "It's a really smart tool that can write, explain, brainstorm, and even problem-solve."

What makes ChatGPT so special? It's designed to understand natural language—how we talk and write—which means you don't need to speak "computer" to use it. Whether you need help drafting an email, creating content, or even planning your next big project, ChatGPT can step in and lend a hand.

Here's just a taste of what it can do:

- **Write Content:** Emails, blog posts, social media captions, you name it.
- **Answer Questions:** From explaining complex topics to giving quick how-to advice.
- **Brainstorm Ideas:** Need fresh ideas for a project? ChatGPT can help.
- **Summarize Information:** Got a long article or report to digest? Ask ChatGPT for a summary.
- **Translate Language:** Need something in another language? It's got your back.

The key is knowing how to communicate with it—and that's where the magic happens.

How to Ask the Right Questions (AKA Prompt Engineering)

Now, let's talk about the secret sauce to using ChatGPT effectively: **prompt engineering.**

What's that, you ask? It's just a fancy way of saying, "How to ask questions in a way that gets you the answers you need." Think of it like this: if you ask vague, unclear questions, you'll get vague, unclear answers. But if you're specific and detailed, ChatGPT can work wonders.

Here's a quick cheat sheet for crafting better prompts:

1. **Be Specific:** Instead of saying, "Write something about marketing," try, "Write a 200-word introduction for a blog post about social media marketing for small businesses."
2. **Set the Context:** Let ChatGPT know who the audience is and what you're aiming for. For example, "Draft a professional email to a client requesting a meeting to discuss project updates."
3. **Give Examples:** If you have a specific tone or format in mind, tell it! For instance, "Write a friendly email like this: 'Hi [Name], I hope you're doing well! I wanted to check in about...'"
4. **Iterate and Adjust:** If the first response isn't quite right, refine your prompt. Think of it as a back-and-forth conversation.

Pro Tip: Don't be afraid to experiment. ChatGPT won't get frustrated if you ask it the same thing five different ways. It's here to help!

Real-Life Examples of ChatGPT in Action

Okay, enough theory. Let's get into the fun part—what ChatGPT can actually do for you. Here are a few real-world examples where this tool shines:

---

1. Writing Professional Email Templates

Let's say you need to send an email to a potential client, but you're not sure how to phrase it without sounding too pushy or too formal. Here's how ChatGPT can help:

Prompt:
"Write a professional yet friendly email to a potential client introducing my web design services. Keep it under 150 words."

Result:
Hi [Client's Name],
I hope this email finds you well! My name is [Your Name], and I specialize in creating user-friendly, visually stunning websites for businesses like yours. I've noticed how [specific compliment about their business, e.g., 'your products have such a strong visual appeal'] and thought a refreshed web presence could help amplify your brand even further.

I'd love to chat about how I can help bring your vision to life. Let me know if you're available for a quick call—I'm happy to work around your schedule!

Looking forward to hearing from you,
[Your Name]

Why It Works: ChatGPT nails the balance between professionalism and approachability, saving you the headache of staring at a blank screen.

---

2. Providing Creative Ideas and Brainstorming Support

Ever been stuck in a rut trying to come up with fresh ideas? Whether it's for a marketing campaign, a blog post, or even a new product, ChatGPT can give your creativity a boost.

Prompt:
"I'm planning a social media campaign to promote a new fitness app. Can you suggest 5 creative ideas to engage users?"

Result:

1. **Challenge of the Week:** Create weekly fitness challenges (e.g., "7-Day Step Challenge") and encourage users to share their progress on social media using a branded hashtag.
2. **User Spotlight:** Feature real users sharing their fitness journeys with the app.
3. **Live Workouts:** Host Instagram or Facebook Live sessions with professional trainers using the app.
4. **Interactive Polls:** Post polls and quizzes about fitness habits, encouraging engagement.
5. **Countdown Giveaway:** Launch a giveaway campaign leading up to the app's release, with prizes for participants who share your posts.

Why It Works: ChatGPT generates creative, actionable ideas in seconds, giving you a starting point to work from.

---

3. Optimizing Daily Workflows

AI isn't just about the big tasks—it's also great for streamlining your day-to-day routine.

For example, let's say you want to plan your day more efficiently.

Prompt:
"Help me create a daily schedule for a freelance writer balancing 3 client projects, a weekly blog post, and time for marketing."

Result:
8:00 AM - 9:00 AM: Check and respond to emails.
9:00 AM - 11:00 AM: Work on Client Project 1 (priority task).
11:00 AM - 11:30 AM: Take a coffee break or do light research for upcoming projects.
11:30 AM - 1:00 PM: Write and edit blog post content for the week.
1:00 PM - 2:00 PM: Lunch break.
2:00 PM - 4:00 PM: Focus on Client Project 2.
4:00 PM - 4:30 PM: Marketing tasks (social media updates, client outreach).
4:30 PM - 5:30 PM: Work on Client Project 3.
5:30 PM: Wrap up and set priorities for tomorrow.

Why It Works: It's like having a productivity coach who helps you stay on track and balance competing demands.

Why ChatGPT and Similar Tools Are Worth It

At the end of the day, tools like ChatGPT aren't just convenient—they're empowering. They take the guesswork out of writing, brainstorming, and planning, freeing you up to focus on what really matters. Whether you're drafting an email, planning your schedule, or looking for the next big idea, these tools save time, reduce stress, and make your life a whole lot easier.

And remember, ChatGPT isn't perfect—it's just a tool. The magic happens when *you* combine your creativity and expertise with its capabilities. Together, you can tackle even the toughest projects.

In the next chapter, we'll dive into how you can take this power to the next level by automating tasks and connecting AI tools to create seamless workflows. Ready? Let's go!

Chapter 5: Automating Your Tasks with AI

Let's be honest for a second: nobody dreams about spending hours on repetitive, boring tasks like organizing emails, updating spreadsheets, or setting reminders. These are the kinds of things that suck up your time and energy—time and energy you could be spending on bigger, more meaningful work. The good news? You don't have to do it all yourself anymore.

AI-powered task automation is like having a personal assistant that never sleeps, never forgets, and never makes excuses. It's not just about saving time (though it will)—it's about freeing yourself from the busywork so you can focus on what actually matters. Let's explore how this works and, more importantly, how you can start automating your daily grind today.

What Is Task Automation?

Task automation is exactly what it sounds like: using technology to perform repetitive tasks automatically, without you having to do them manually. It's like putting your work on autopilot. Instead of spending hours each week on small, time-consuming chores, you let AI and automation tools handle them for you.

Here's a simple example:
Imagine you receive a client inquiry via email. Normally, you'd manually copy their information into a spreadsheet, send them a follow-up email, and maybe even set a reminder to check in with them later. With task automation, you can set up a system where:

1. The email automatically gets added to your spreadsheet.
2. A personalized follow-up email is sent immediately.

3. A reminder is created in your task manager for next week.

All of this happens without you lifting a finger. Magic, right?

Connecting Your Workflow with Tools Like Zapier

One of the best tools to help you automate tasks is **Zapier**. Think of Zapier as the middleman that connects all your favorite apps and makes them talk to each other. Whether you're using Google Sheets, Slack, Asana, or any of the thousands of apps Zapier supports, you can create "Zaps" (automations) to streamline your workflow.

Here's how it works in simple terms:

- **Trigger**: Something happens in one app (e.g., you receive a new email).
- **Action**: Zapier automatically performs an action in another app (e.g., it adds the email to your task list).

What makes Zapier awesome?

- It doesn't require any coding skills.
- It works with thousands of apps, so you can connect pretty much anything.
- It's customizable, meaning you can design workflows that fit your unique needs.

Real-Life Examples of Task Automation with AI

Let me show you how automation tools like Zapier (and similar ones like Automate.io) can simplify your day.

---

1. Automatically Organize Emails and Create Task Lists

We've all been there: an inbox overflowing with emails, and most of them require some kind of follow-up or action. It's overwhelming, right? Here's how automation can help.

Scenario:
You receive client inquiries via email, and you need to:

- Log their details in a spreadsheet.
- Send a personalized follow-up email.
- Add a task to your project management tool to review their request later.

Automation Workflow:

- **Trigger**: A new email with a specific subject line or keyword arrives in your inbox.
- **Action 1**: Zapier extracts the email sender's name, email address, and inquiry details and adds them to a Google Sheet.
- **Action 2**: A follow-up email is automatically sent, thanking them for reaching out and confirming you'll respond soon.

- **Action 3**: A new task is created in Asana (or any task management app you use) to review their request.

Why It Works:
This workflow eliminates the manual steps of sorting emails, copying data, and creating tasks. You get everything organized instantly, and nothing slips through the cracks.

---

2. Syncing Data Across Platforms

Let's say you're juggling multiple apps to run your business—Google Sheets for tracking data, Slack for communication, and Trello for project management. Keeping everything updated manually can feel like a full-time job.

Scenario:
You're tracking sales leads in Google Sheets but also need them added as tasks in Trello and shared with your team on Slack.

Automation Workflow:

- **Trigger**: A new row is added to your Google Sheet.
- **Action 1**: Zapier creates a new task in Trello with all the details from the spreadsheet.
- **Action 2**: A message is sent to your team on Slack, letting them know about the new lead.

Why It Works:
Instead of updating three separate tools every time something changes, this automation ensures everything stays synced. You save time and avoid the frustration of missing updates.

---

3. Simplifying Calendar Management

If you've ever spent way too much time scheduling meetings, you know how frustrating it can be. Automating your calendar is a lifesaver.

Scenario:
You want to streamline how people book meetings with you, avoid double-bookings, and automatically follow up afterward.

Automation Workflow:

- **Trigger**: Someone schedules a meeting using a tool like Calendly.
- **Action 1**: The meeting is added to your Google Calendar with all the details.
- **Action 2**: A follow-up email is automatically sent 24 hours after the meeting to thank them and provide next steps.

Why It Works:
You eliminate the back-and-forth of scheduling and ensure every meeting ends with a professional follow-up.

Getting Started with Automation

If you're new to automation, don't worry—it's easier than you think. Here's how to get started:

1. **Identify Your Repetitive Tasks**
   Take a moment to think about the tasks you do over and over again. It could be sorting emails, updating spreadsheets, or creating reminders. These are perfect candidates for automation.
2. **Choose the Right Tools**
   Start with a beginner-friendly tool like Zapier or Automate.io. Both have free versions that let you experiment without any risk.
3. **Start Small**
   Pick one simple workflow to automate. For example, set up a Zap to log new emails into a spreadsheet. Once you're comfortable, you can build more complex automations.
4. **Test and Refine**
   Automation isn't always perfect right out of the gate. Test your workflows, tweak them as needed, and don't be afraid to experiment.

Why This Matters

Here's the thing: automation isn't just a nice-to-have—it's a productivity superpower. When you automate the small stuff, you free up mental space and energy for the big stuff. You're no longer stuck in the weeds of your day-to-day tasks, which means you can focus on creative projects, strategic thinking, or just taking a well-deserved break.

And the best part? You don't need to be a tech wizard to make it happen. Tools like Zapier make automation accessible to anyone, no coding required. So, go ahead and try it out—you'll be amazed at how much time you'll get back.

In the next chapter, we'll explore how AI tools can take your time management skills to the next level. Spoiler alert: it's about more than just to-do lists. Let's keep going!

Chapter 6: Time Management with AI

Let's face it: no matter how hard we try, we all get the same 24 hours in a day. The difference between feeling accomplished and feeling overwhelmed often comes down to how well we manage our time. If you're anything like me, you've probably spent way too much time juggling calendars, making endless to-do lists, and wondering where all your time went by the end of the day.

This is where AI steps in. AI-powered tools can help you take control of your schedule, optimize your workflow, and make every minute count. In this chapter, I'll show you how AI can revolutionize your approach to time management—not by adding more to your plate, but by making sure you're focusing on what really matters.

How AI Can Help You Organize Your Schedule

If you've ever struggled to coordinate meetings, manage deadlines, or figure out when you'll have time to actually do the work, you're not alone. These are exactly the kinds of problems that AI-powered scheduling tools were built to solve.

Smart Calendars
AI-enabled calendars like Google Calendar and Microsoft Outlook aren't just about setting reminders—they're practically personal assistants. For example:

- They can **analyze your availability** and suggest the best times for meetings based on your existing commitments.
- Tools like **Calendly** go a step further by automating the scheduling process entirely. Just send someone your link, and the tool will find the perfect time slot without all the back-and-forth emails.

AI-Powered Task Prioritization
AI doesn't just help you schedule tasks; it helps you prioritize them. Apps like **Motion** automatically analyze your to-do list, figure out the most urgent tasks, and block time for them on your calendar. It's like having a productivity coach keeping your day on track.

Why It Works:
Instead of wasting time figuring out when and how to get things done, these tools do the thinking for you. They turn scheduling into a simple, stress-free process.

Analyzing Work Habits with AI to Maximize Efficiency

Have you ever looked back on your day and thought, "What exactly did I do today?" It's easy to lose track of how we spend our time, especially when distractions and interruptions keep pulling us in different directions. This is where AI's ability to analyze your habits becomes a game-changer.

Tracking Your Time
Tools like **RescueTime** and **Clockify** use AI to track how you spend your hours. They categorize your activities—email, meetings, focused work, social media—and provide insights on where your time is going. It's like having a mirror that shows you exactly how productive (or not) you've been.

Identifying Patterns
Once AI tools start tracking your habits, they can help you spot trends. For example:

- Do you get more done in the morning or the afternoon?

- Are meetings eating into your time for deep, focused work?
- How often are you distracted by non-essential tasks?

Making Data-Driven Adjustments
Once you know where your time is going, you can make smarter decisions. AI tools can suggest changes, like blocking time for focused work during your most productive hours or scheduling breaks to avoid burnout.

Why It Works:
AI doesn't just show you how you're spending your time—it helps you take back control and use it more wisely.

Real-Life Examples: AI Tools for Time Management

Let's get practical. Here are a couple of real-world examples of how AI can make a difference in your daily routine.

---

1. Creating a Daily Schedule with AI

If you're juggling multiple tasks, it's easy to feel overwhelmed by competing priorities. This is where AI tools shine.

Example Tool: Motion
Motion combines your calendar, to-do list, and priorities into one seamless system. Here's how it works:

1. You enter your tasks and deadlines into the app.
2. The AI analyzes your calendar to find open time slots.
3. It automatically creates a detailed schedule that ensures you stay on track without overloading yourself.

Real-Life Scenario:
Imagine you're a freelance designer balancing three client projects, daily emails, and a personal goal to write a weekly blog post. Motion might create a schedule like this:

- **8:00 AM - 9:00 AM:** Check and respond to emails.
- **9:00 AM - 11:00 AM:** Work on Client A's project.
- **11:00 AM - 11:30 AM:** Coffee break and light planning.
- **11:30 AM - 1:00 PM:** Brainstorm ideas for your blog post.
- **1:00 PM - 2:00 PM:** Lunch.
- **2:00 PM - 4:00 PM:** Client B's project.
- **4:00 PM - 5:00 PM:** Client C's project.
- **5:00 PM:** Wrap-up and review priorities for tomorrow.

Why It Works:
Instead of feeling like you have too much on your plate, you get a clear, realistic plan for the day.

---

2. Boosting Meeting Efficiency with AI Assistants

Meetings can be a major time suck—especially when they run longer than necessary or fail to achieve clear outcomes. AI-powered meeting assistants can help you get more value from your time.

Example Tools: Notion AI and Otter.ai

- **Notion AI** helps you prep for meetings by summarizing key documents, organizing agendas, and even suggesting action items.
- **Otter.ai** transcribes meetings in real time, so you don't have to frantically take notes. After the meeting, it creates a summary of key points and action items.

Real-Life Scenario:
You're leading a weekly team meeting and want to ensure everyone's aligned. Here's how AI can help:

1. **Before the meeting:** Notion AI organizes your agenda and highlights discussion points.
2. **During the meeting:** Otter.ai transcribes the conversation in real time, so you can stay focused on leading the discussion.
3. **After the meeting:** Otter.ai generates a summary and sends it to the team, ensuring everyone knows their next steps.

Why It Works:
No more wasted time trying to recall what was said or chasing people for follow-ups. Meetings become shorter, clearer, and more productive.

Why AI Is a Game-Changer for Time Management

At the heart of it, time management is about making choices—deciding what's worth your time and what's not. AI tools help you make those choices smarter, faster, and with less mental effort. They don't just tell you what to do; they make sure you're doing it in the most efficient way possible.

Whether it's creating your daily schedule, analyzing your work habits, or making meetings more productive, AI doesn't just save time—it gives you the freedom to focus on what really matters.

So, instead of trying to squeeze more hours out of the day, why not let AI help you make the most of the hours you already have? In the next chapter, we'll dive into how AI can take your creativity to the next level. Let's keep the momentum going!

Advanced Applications of AI

Chapter 7: Content Creation with AI

If there's one area where AI truly feels like a creative partner, it's content creation. Whether you're a marketer, a small business owner, or just someone trying to keep up with the endless demand for engaging content, AI can make your life a whole lot easier. And no, it's not about letting AI take over your voice or creativity—it's about using it to save time, spark ideas, and polish your work to perfection.

In this chapter, I'll walk you through how AI can help you create high-quality content, both written and visual, faster than ever before. From crafting killer social media captions to generating professional-looking reports, you'll see how AI can transform the way you approach content creation.

Writing High-Quality Articles and Reports with AI

Let's start with the written word. We've all been there: staring at a blank page, waiting for inspiration to strike. Or worse, scrambling to finish a report under a tight deadline, wishing there was an easier way. With AI tools like ChatGPT, Jasper, and others, you can go from idea to finished product in a fraction of the time.

Here's how you can use AI to create compelling written content:

1. **Brainstorming Ideas:**
   AI is perfect for breaking through writer's block.

Need a fresh angle for a blog post? Just ask. For example:
Prompt: “What are some unique topics for a blog post about sustainable fashion?”
Result: AI will generate a list of ideas like “10 Ways to Build a Sustainable Wardrobe on a Budget” or “How Fast Fashion is Impacting the Environment.”

2. **Drafting Content:**
   You don’t need to start from scratch. AI can create a rough draft based on your instructions. For example:
   Prompt: “Write a 500-word article about the benefits of remote work for small businesses.”
   Result: You’ll get a structured draft that you can refine and personalize.
3. **Editing and Polishing:**
   Already have a draft? AI can help you improve it. Tools like Grammarly or ChatGPT can suggest edits for grammar, tone, and readability. For example, you can say:
   Prompt: “Rewrite this paragraph to make it sound more professional.”
4. **Creating Long-Form Reports:**
   AI can assist with formatting and organizing complex documents like business reports.
   Prompt: “Draft a report summarizing the key findings of a survey on customer satisfaction, including an introduction, key data points, and recommendations.”
   Result: You’ll have a professional-looking report template ready to customize.

Pro Tip: AI isn't perfect, so always review and revise the output. Think of it as a collaborator, not a replacement for your creativity or expertise.

Generating Visual Content with AI (Canva, DALL·E, and More)

Now let's talk about visuals. Whether you're designing social media graphics, creating presentations, or brainstorming ad concepts, visual content is a must. But let's be real—not all of us are graphic designers. That's where AI-powered tools like **Canva** and **DALL·E** come in.

Canva: AI for Design

Canva is already a favorite for its easy drag-and-drop design features, but its AI tools take it to the next level.

- **AI-Powered Suggestions:** Canva can recommend templates, color palettes, and layouts based on your brand or project needs.
- **Text-to-Image AI:** Canva now includes features that let you generate unique images based on a description. For example, you can type "modern minimalist logo with a green leaf" and get a custom design.

DALL·E: AI for Unique Images

DALL·E, developed by OpenAI, is like the Picasso of AI. It creates original, one-of-a-kind images based on text prompts.

- **Example Prompt:** "A futuristic cityscape at sunset, painted in watercolor."
- **Result:** DALL·E will generate stunning visuals that you can use for presentations, blog posts, or ads.

Why It Works: These tools give you professional-looking visuals without needing advanced design skills. Plus, they're great for creating content that stands out—no more generic stock photos.

Real-Life Examples: Content Marketing with AI

Let's get into some real-world applications. Whether you're working on a big content strategy or just trying to impress a client, AI can help you shine.

---

1. AI-Driven Content Marketing: From Social Media to Long-Form Articles

Imagine you're launching a new product and need a full content marketing campaign. Here's how AI can help:

- **Social Media Posts:**
  Prompt: "Write a catchy Instagram caption for a new

eco-friendly water bottle."
Result:
"Stay hydrated and save the planet 🌍. Meet your new favorite water bottle—made from 100% recycled materials. 💧 #EcoFriendlyLiving"

- **Blog Posts:**
  Prompt: "Write a 1,000-word blog post about the importance of staying hydrated, including health benefits and tips for drinking more water."
  Result: A detailed draft with facts, tips, and a strong call-to-action to buy your product.
- **Email Campaigns:**
  Prompt: "Create an email subject line and body text to promote our new water bottle."
  Result:
  Subject Line: "Your Perfect Water Bottle is Here 💧"
  Body:
  "We're excited to introduce our eco-friendly water bottle. Lightweight, durable, and sustainable—it's everything you need to stay hydrated on the go. Order yours today and join the movement for a greener future."

---

2. Creating Client Proposal Templates with AI

Let's say you're a freelancer or consultant, and you need to send a polished proposal to a potential client. Instead of starting from scratch, AI can help you create a professional, customized template.

Scenario:
You're pitching a social media strategy to a new client.

Prompt:
"Write a client proposal template for a social media strategy, including sections for an introduction, goals, deliverables, timeline, and pricing."

Result:

- **Introduction:** A personalized overview of your expertise and the client's needs.
- **Goals:** Specific, measurable objectives (e.g., increase Instagram engagement by 30% in three months).
- **Deliverables:** A clear breakdown of what you'll provide, such as content calendars, analytics reports, and ad campaigns.
- **Timeline:** A step-by-step plan with deadlines.
- **Pricing:** A transparent, professional fee structure.

You can easily tweak the template to match each client's unique needs.

Why It Works: AI saves you hours while ensuring your proposals look polished and professional—perfect for impressing clients.

Why AI is a Must-Have for Content Creation

Creating high-quality content doesn't have to be stressful or time-consuming. With AI, you have a creative partner that can:

- Help you brainstorm ideas and get past writer's block.
- Save time by generating drafts, templates, and visuals in minutes.
- Take the guesswork out of designing professional-looking graphics and reports.

The best part? AI doesn't replace your creativity—it enhances it. By handling the time-consuming tasks, AI frees you up to focus on strategy, storytelling, and connecting with your audience.

In the next chapter, we'll explore how AI can take your data analysis to the next level, helping you make smarter, faster decisions. Let's keep the momentum going!

Chapter 8: AI for Data Analysis

Let me guess—when you hear the words "data analysis," your first thought is probably something like, *Ugh, spreadsheets.* Trust me, I get it. Diving into rows and rows of numbers isn't exactly most people's idea of fun. But here's the thing: understanding your data is essential for making smarter decisions, whether you're running a business, managing a team, or just trying to optimize your side hustle.

Here's the good news: AI tools make data analysis faster, easier, and, dare I say it, kind of exciting. They take the heavy lifting out of crunching numbers and turn raw data into actionable insights—all without you needing a degree in statistics. In this chapter, I'll show you how AI can transform the way you analyze data and make decisions.

An Introduction to AI-Powered Data Analysis Tools

AI-driven tools like Tableau and Power BI are designed to take your data from "What does this even mean?" to "Oh, I see exactly what's happening here!" Let's take a quick look at these tools and what they can do for you.

1. Tableau

- Tableau is a powerhouse when it comes to creating interactive dashboards and visualizations.
- It allows you to connect to various data sources (spreadsheets, databases, APIs) and transforms your data into stunning visual insights.
- Tableau's AI features, like "Explain Data," can automatically generate explanations for trends and anomalies in your charts.

2. Power BI

- Power BI, a Microsoft product, is perfect for businesses of all sizes.
- It integrates seamlessly with tools like Excel, SQL databases, and even cloud platforms.
- With AI-powered features like "Quick Insights," Power BI can highlight key patterns and trends in your data at the click of a button.

3. Other Tools Worth Mentioning

- **Google Data Studio:** A free, user-friendly option for creating reports and dashboards.
- **Qlik Sense:** Another powerful tool for analyzing and visualizing data with AI insights.

Why These Tools Matter: They take data that might seem overwhelming or boring and turn it into something visual, digestible, and actionable. Instead of staring at endless columns, you're looking at charts, graphs, and dashboards that actually make sense.

How AI Extracts Insights from Complex Data

Here's where AI shines: it doesn't just organize your data; it helps you *understand* it. AI tools can spot trends, identify outliers, and even make predictions—all things that would take you hours (or days) to figure out manually.

1. Identifying Trends and Patterns

Let's say you're tracking sales data for your business. AI can quickly highlight:

- Which products are performing best.
- Which days of the week generate the most sales.
- Seasonal trends you might not have noticed.

Instead of digging through spreadsheets, AI tools present this information visually, so you can see the bigger picture at a glance.

2. Detecting Anomalies

Sometimes, the most important insights come from things that *don't* follow the trend—like a sudden dip in sales or an unexpected spike in website traffic. AI tools can flag these anomalies automatically, so you can investigate what's going on.

3. Making Predictions

AI isn't just about analyzing the past—it's also about looking ahead. Predictive analytics uses historical data to forecast future trends. For example:

- If you're running an e-commerce store, AI can predict which products will sell best next month.
- If you're managing a team, AI can help you anticipate workload bottlenecks before they happen.

Why It Works: AI handles the number-crunching, so you can focus on making informed decisions based on the insights it provides.

Real-Life Examples: AI in Action for Data Analysis

Let's put theory into practice. Here are two examples of how AI-powered data analysis can make a real difference in your work.

---

1. Analyzing Sales Data with AI

Scenario:
You're managing a small retail business, and you want to understand how your sales are trending across different products and locations.

How AI Helps:

- **Step 1:** Import your sales data into Power BI or Tableau.
- **Step 2:** Use AI features like "Quick Insights" (Power BI) or "Explain Data" (Tableau) to automatically highlight patterns.
- **Step 3:** Generate visualizations, like bar charts showing top-performing products or heat maps showing regional sales differences.

Example Insights:

- You notice that sales for a specific product spike on weekends.
- You see that one location is underperforming compared to others, prompting you to investigate further.
- You identify a seasonal trend that suggests stocking up on certain products before the holidays.

Why It Works: Instead of spending hours digging through spreadsheets, you get a clear picture of what's working and what needs attention—all in minutes.

---

2. Creating Data-Driven Reports and Visual Dashboards

Scenario:
You've been asked to present a quarterly performance report to your team or clients. Normally, this would mean hours of manual work compiling data, creating charts, and formatting slides.

How AI Helps:

- **Step 1:** Pull data from multiple sources (e.g., Google Analytics, sales software, marketing tools) into a tool like Tableau.
- **Step 2:** Use AI to create dynamic visualizations that update automatically when new data comes in.

- **Step 3:** Export your dashboard or embed it into your presentation software for a professional, polished look.

Example Visuals:

- A pie chart showing revenue breakdown by product category.
- A line graph tracking website traffic and conversions over the quarter.
- A heatmap highlighting geographic regions with the highest customer engagement.

Why It Works: Your report looks professional and data-driven, and the best part? The dashboard stays updated in real time, so you're always ready for the next presentation.

Why AI for Data Analysis Is a Game-Changer

Here's the thing about data: it's not about having more of it—it's about knowing what to do with it. That's where AI comes in. These tools make data accessible, actionable, and even fun (yes, fun).

By using AI for data analysis, you:

- Save hours of manual effort.
- Gain deeper insights that might otherwise go unnoticed.

- Make smarter decisions based on real, actionable data.

And the best part? You don't need to be a data scientist to use these tools. Whether you're running a business, managing a team, or simply trying to optimize your own performance, AI gives you the power to make sense of your data—and make better decisions because of it.

In the next chapter, we'll explore how AI can help you manage customer relationships and improve client experiences. Spoiler alert: it's more than just chatbots. Let's dive in!

Chapter 9: AI for Customer Relationship Management

If there's one thing that can make or break a business, it's customer relationships. Whether you're running a small business, managing a sales team, or growing your side hustle, keeping your customers happy and engaged is key. But let's face it: managing customer relationships can be overwhelming. There are emails to respond to, leads to follow up with, data to track, and let's not forget—actually delivering the product or service you promised.

This is where AI in customer relationship management (CRM) tools steps in. It's like having an assistant who not only organizes your customer data but also helps you make smarter, faster decisions. In this chapter, I'll show you how AI-powered CRM tools can save you time, predict customer behavior, and even help you deliver a better customer experience.

How CRM Tools Integrate AI Features

Let's start with the basics: CRM tools are designed to help you track, manage, and nurture customer relationships. But with AI, they go from being simple databases to powerful, decision-making assistants.

Popular AI-Enabled CRM Tools

1. **Salesforce AI (Einstein):**
   - Salesforce's Einstein AI is like having a data scientist built into your CRM. It analyzes customer data, predicts sales opportunities, and even automates tasks like lead scoring and follow-ups.
2. **HubSpot:**
   - HubSpot uses AI to track customer interactions, automate email responses, and provide insights on how to engage leads effectively. Plus, it integrates seamlessly with marketing tools to streamline your campaigns.
3. **Zoho CRM:**
   - Zoho's AI assistant, Zia, can answer questions about your data, detect patterns,

and even suggest the best time to contact leads.

4. **Pipedrive:**
    - Pipedrive uses AI to prioritize deals, identify at-risk opportunities, and recommend actions to close more sales.

Why AI-Enabled CRM Matters:
These tools aren't just about storing customer data. They help you analyze it, understand your customers' needs, and act on insights—all while automating the repetitive tasks that would otherwise eat up your day.

Using AI to Predict Customer Behavior and Optimize Experiences

Here's where AI really shines: it doesn't just show you what's happening with your customers—it helps you anticipate what they'll do next. This is called predictive analytics, and it's a game-changer for customer management.

1. Predicting Customer Behavior

AI tools analyze your customer data (like purchase history, website behavior, and email interactions) to predict things like:

- **Likelihood to Buy:** Which leads are most likely to convert into paying customers?
- **Churn Risk:** Which customers are at risk of leaving, so you can take action to retain them?
- **Upsell Opportunities:** Which customers might be interested in upgrading or buying additional products?

2. Optimizing Customer Experiences

AI also helps you tailor experiences to individual customers. For example:

- Personalizing email campaigns based on customer preferences.
- Recommending products or services based on past purchases.
- Adjusting marketing messages based on where a customer is in their journey (e.g., new lead vs. loyal customer).

Why It Works: Customers expect personalized, seamless experiences. AI makes it possible to deliver this at scale—something that would be impossible to do manually.

Real-Life Examples: AI in Action for CRM

Now let's look at a couple of real-world examples where AI-powered CRM tools can make a tangible difference.

---

1. Automating Customer Support with AI

Scenario:
You're running an online business, and you're drowning in customer emails. Many of them ask the same basic questions, like "What's your return policy?" or "How long does shipping take?"

Solution:
Use an AI-powered chatbot or CRM tool to handle these inquiries automatically.

How It Works:

- **Step 1:** Set up an AI chatbot (like HubSpot's chatbot or Zendesk AI) to respond to FAQs.
- **Step 2:** Train the bot to recognize common customer questions and provide accurate answers.
- **Step 3:** If the bot can't handle a question, it escalates the issue to a human team member.

Result:

- Customers get instant responses, 24/7.
- Your team spends less time answering repetitive questions and more time solving complex issues.

Why It Works:
Quick responses make customers feel valued, and

automating repetitive tasks frees up your team to focus on higher-priority work.

---

2. Improving Customer Retention with Predictive Analytics

Scenario:
You run a subscription-based service, and you've noticed that some customers cancel after a few months. You want to reduce churn and keep more customers around.

Solution:
Use a CRM tool with AI-powered churn prediction to identify at-risk customers.

How It Works:

- **Step 1:** Your CRM analyzes customer behavior, like login frequency, support interactions, and payment history.
- **Step 2:** The AI flags customers who are at high risk of canceling their subscriptions.
- **Step 3:** You create targeted retention campaigns—like offering a discount, checking in personally, or suggesting additional features to improve their experience.

Result:

- Fewer cancellations and higher customer satisfaction.
- A proactive approach to retention, rather than reacting after it's too late.

Why It Works:
By identifying and addressing issues before they lead to cancellations, you can improve retention rates and build stronger relationships with your customers.

Why AI for CRM Is a Must-Have

Managing customer relationships is no small task, but AI makes it not only manageable but scalable. Here's why it matters:

1. **Save Time:** AI handles the repetitive tasks—like responding to FAQs or updating customer records—so you can focus on high-value activities.
2. **Make Smarter Decisions:** With predictive analytics, you can understand what your customers need before they even ask.
3. **Deliver Better Experiences:** Personalized, timely interactions make customers feel seen and valued, which builds loyalty and trust.

Whether you're a solopreneur juggling dozens of clients or part of a team managing thousands, AI-powered CRM tools are your secret weapon for staying organized, proactive, and customer-focused.

In the next chapter, we'll explore how AI can help you develop ethical, transparent practices while ensuring data privacy—a crucial topic as AI becomes more integrated into our lives. Let's keep going!

Ensuring the Successful Use of AI Tools

Chapter 10: Choosing the Right AI Tools for You

Let's be honest: the world of AI tools can feel like an overwhelming buffet. There's so much on the menu that it's hard to know where to start. From language models to automation platforms to data analysis software, the options are endless—and they all promise to save you time, boost your productivity, and maybe even make your coffee (okay, not quite).

But here's the thing: not every tool is worth your time or money. Choosing the right AI tools isn't about grabbing the shiniest one on the shelf; it's about finding the ones that genuinely fit your needs, your workflow, and your goals. In this chapter, I'll walk you through how to choose the perfect tools for your unique situation, without wasting time or budget on things you don't need.

A Guide to Choosing AI Tools for Different Work Scenarios

First things first: the "best" AI tool depends on what you're trying to achieve. Let's break it down by common work scenarios and the tools that are best suited for each one.

1. Content Creation

- **Your Goal:** Writing articles, creating marketing copy, or designing visuals.
- **Recommended Tools:**
  - **ChatGPT or Jasper**: For generating blog posts, emails, and social media captions.
  - **Canva**: For creating professional-looking graphics and presentations.
  - **DALL·E**: For generating custom, AI-created images based on text prompts.

2. Task Automation

- **Your Goal:** Automating repetitive tasks and streamlining your workflows.
- **Recommended Tools:**
  - **Zapier**: Connects your apps and automates workflows (e.g., syncing emails with your task manager).
  - **Automate.io**: A simpler alternative to Zapier for automating workflows.

- Calendly: For scheduling meetings without the back-and-forth emails.

3. Data Analysis

- **Your Goal:** Turning raw data into actionable insights.
- **Recommended Tools:**
    - **Power BI**: For creating data visualizations and reports.
    - **Tableau**: For interactive dashboards and deep data analysis.
    - **Google Data Studio**: A free, user-friendly option for combining and visualizing data.

4. Customer Relationship Management (CRM)

- **Your Goal:** Managing customer interactions and improving retention.
- **Recommended Tools:**
    - **Salesforce AI (Einstein)**: For predictive analytics and lead scoring.
    - **HubSpot CRM**: For automating email follow-ups and tracking customer interactions.
    - **Zoho CRM (Zia)**: For actionable insights and AI-driven suggestions.

5. Personal Productivity

- **Your Goal:** Managing your time and staying organized.

- **Recommended Tools:**
  - **Notion AI**: For organizing your tasks, notes, and projects with the help of AI.
  - **Motion**: Combines scheduling, to-do lists, and time management into one tool.
  - **RescueTime**: Tracks your time usage and provides insights into your productivity habits.

How to Evaluate the Cost-Effectiveness of AI Tools

Not every AI tool is worth the price tag. Some are overhyped, others are overpriced, and a few might be both. Here's how to evaluate whether a tool is worth the investment:

1. Start with a Free Trial

Most AI tools offer free trials or freemium versions. Take advantage of these to test the tool before committing. During the trial, ask yourself:

- Does this tool solve a specific problem I have?
- Is it easy to use, or is there a steep learning curve?
- Does it integrate with the tools I'm already using?

2. Compare Features vs. Cost

Don't just look at the price—look at what you're getting for it.

- Are the features practical for your needs, or are you paying for bells and whistles you'll never use?
- If a tool has a lower-cost competitor with similar features, does the higher-priced tool offer something extra that's worth paying for?

3. Time Saved = Money Saved

A good way to evaluate the ROI (return on investment) of an AI tool is to calculate how much time it saves you. For example:

- If a tool saves you 5 hours a week, multiply that by your hourly rate to estimate its value.
- If the tool costs less than the time it saves, it's a good investment.

4. Scalability

Think about whether the tool will grow with you. A tool that works for your current needs might not be sufficient as your workload or business expands. Look for tools that offer scalable plans or features.

How to Avoid Blindly Using AI Tools

It's easy to fall into the trap of thinking, *If it's AI, it must be amazing.* But here's the truth: not every AI tool is worth using, and some might even create more problems than they solve. Here's how to avoid wasting time and energy:

1. Define Your Problem First

Before you even start researching tools, ask yourself:

- What problem am I trying to solve?
- What's my goal for using AI in this specific area?

For example, if you're drowning in repetitive admin tasks, a tool like Zapier might be a great fit. But if your goal is to improve customer engagement, a CRM tool with AI-powered features would be more relevant.

2. Don't Get Distracted by Hype

Just because a tool is trending or has flashy marketing doesn't mean it's right for you. Focus on your needs, not the tool's popularity.

3. Keep It Simple

The best AI tools are the ones you'll actually use. If a tool feels overly complex or doesn't fit into your existing workflow, it's probably not the right choice.

4. Watch Out for Over-Automation

While automation is a huge time-saver, over-automating can lead to problems. For example:

- Sending overly robotic emails can alienate customers.

- Automating processes you don't fully understand can create errors.

Use AI as a helper, not as a replacement for human oversight and judgment.

Why Choosing the Right AI Tools Matters

Here's the thing: the right AI tool can save you hours of work, reduce stress, and make your life so much easier. But the wrong tool? It can waste your time, blow your budget, and leave you feeling frustrated.

By taking the time to choose tools that align with your goals and workflow, you'll get the most out of what AI has to offer—without the headaches. And remember, it's okay to start small. Even one well-chosen AI tool can make a big difference in your productivity and efficiency.

In the next chapter, we'll dive into how to improve your AI skills—because just like any tool, the more you know about how to use it, the better the results you'll get. Let's keep going!

Chapter 11: Improving Your AI Skills: Learning Prompt Engineering

Here's the deal: using AI is like having a superpower. But just like any superpower, how effective it is depends on how well you know how to use it. And when it comes to working with tools like ChatGPT, Jasper, or any other AI system, the secret sauce is **prompt engineering**.

Think of prompts as the instructions you give to the AI. If your instructions are vague or unclear, you'll get results that are just as vague. But if you can master the art of crafting precise, thoughtful prompts, the results can be nothing short of amazing. In this chapter, we'll explore what prompt engineering is, why it matters, and how you can use it to get exactly what you need from your AI tools.

What Is Prompt Engineering, and Why Does It Matter?

At its core, prompt engineering is the process of designing clear, detailed, and effective instructions to guide AI tools. Think of it as having a conversation with the AI—your job is to ask the right questions or give the right context so the AI knows exactly what you're looking for.

Why is this important? Because AI isn't magic. It doesn't "know" what you want unless you tell it, and how you phrase your prompt can make or break the quality of the response. Here's a simple analogy:

Imagine you walk into a restaurant and say, "Give me food." The chef might bring you anything—spaghetti, sushi, or maybe just a salad. But if you say, "I'd like a medium-rare steak with a side of roasted vegetables and a glass of iced tea," you're much more likely to get exactly what you want.

It's the same with AI. The more specific and detailed your prompts are, the better the results you'll get.

Tips and Strategies for Writing Effective Prompts

Now that you know why prompts are so important, let's talk about how to craft them effectively. Here are some strategies that have worked for me (and trust me, I've had my fair share of trial and error):

1. Be Specific

The more details you include, the less guessing the AI has to do. Instead of saying, "Write a blog post about fitness," try something like:

- **Prompt:** "Write a 500-word blog post about the benefits of strength training for beginners. Include three practical tips, a friendly tone, and a call to action at the end."

Why it works: You're giving the AI clear instructions on the length, topic, tone, and structure.

---

2. Provide Context

AI works better when it understands the bigger picture. Let it know who the audience is and what your goal is. For example:

- **Prompt:** “Draft a LinkedIn post targeting small business owners, explaining how AI tools like ChatGPT can save them time on administrative tasks. Use a conversational tone and keep it under 150 words.”

Why it works: You’re helping the AI tailor its response to the right audience and format.

---

3. Break It Into Steps

If the task is complex, break it down into smaller steps. For example:

- **Prompt:** “Step 1: Outline the key sections of a 1,000-word blog post about remote work productivity. Step 2: Expand on the outline with 2-3 sentences per section. Step 3: Add a conclusion with actionable tips.”

Why it works: The AI can focus on one part at a time, resulting in a more organized and coherent output.

---

4. Experiment with Tone and Style

AI can mimic different tones and styles, but you need to ask for it. For example:

- **Prompt (Professional):** "Write a formal email to a client explaining a delay in project delivery. Apologize for the inconvenience and propose a new timeline."
- **Prompt (Casual):** "Draft a friendly email to a client explaining why their project will be a little late. Keep it light and positive, and suggest a new deadline."

Why it works: By specifying the tone, you ensure the response aligns with your communication style.

---

5. Iterate and Refine

Your first prompt might not always get the perfect result—and that's okay. Treat it as a conversation. If the response isn't quite right, adjust your prompt and try again. For example:

- **Initial Prompt:** "Write a summary of this article."
- **Refined Prompt:** "Summarize this article in 3-5 sentences, focusing on the main arguments and excluding minor details."

Why it works: Each refinement brings you closer to the result you're looking for.

Real-Life Examples: Fine-Tuning Prompts for Better Results

Let's look at some real-world scenarios where prompt engineering can take your AI output from "meh" to "wow."

Example 1: Crafting a Social Media Post

Initial Prompt:
"Write a post about a new productivity app."

Result:
The AI generates a generic post that lacks personality or detail.

Refined Prompt:
"Write an engaging Twitter post about a new productivity app called 'FocusPro.' Highlight its time-tracking feature and how it helps users stay organized. Keep it under 280 characters and use a friendly, energetic tone."

Final Output:
"Stay on top of your to-do list with FocusPro! ⏰ This app tracks your time, helps you stay organized, and boosts your productivity. Say goodbye to procrastination and hello to focus! 💪 #TimeManagement #ProductivityApp"

Why It's Better: The refined prompt gives the AI clear instructions on tone, format, and key points to include.

Example 2: Writing a Report Summary

Initial Prompt:
"Summarize this sales report."

Result:
The AI generates a summary that's too vague and skips key details.

Refined Prompt:
"Summarize this sales report in 200 words. Focus on the monthly revenue trends, key product categories, and recommendations for improving next month's performance."

Final Output:
"This month's sales report highlights a 10% increase in revenue compared to last month, driven by strong performance in the electronics category. However, clothing sales saw a slight decline. Recommendations include launching a targeted promotion for clothing and expanding the electronics inventory to meet demand."

Why It's Better: The refined prompt ensures the summary is focused, concise, and actionable.

Example 3: Brainstorming Ideas

Initial Prompt:
"Suggest blog topics about AI."

Result:
The AI generates a generic list of topics that are either too broad or unoriginal.

Refined Prompt:
"Suggest 10 blog topics about AI for small business owners. Focus on practical, actionable advice, and include topics that highlight time-saving and cost-cutting benefits."

Final Output:

1. "5 AI Tools Every Small Business Should Use to Save Time"
2. "How AI Can Automate Your Daily Tasks and Boost Productivity"
3. "Using AI to Create Marketing Campaigns That Work"

   ...

Why It's Better: The refined prompt provides a specific audience and goal, resulting in more relevant and useful ideas.

Why Learning Prompt Engineering Is Worth Your Time

Here's the bottom line: AI is only as good as the instructions you give it. By learning how to write effective prompts, you're not just using AI—you're mastering it. This skill will save you time, improve the quality of your outputs, and make you feel like a pro every time you interact with AI tools.

Think of prompt engineering as the bridge between your ideas and the AI's capabilities. With a little practice, you'll be crafting prompts that get you exactly what you need, every time.

In the next chapter, we'll explore how to navigate the ethical and privacy challenges that come with using AI tools responsibly. Because as much as AI can do, it's still up to us to use it wisely. Let's dive in!

第五大章

Chapter 12: Ethics and Privacy in Using AI Tools

Let's take a step back for a moment. We've talked about all the incredible things AI can do—saving time, boosting productivity, and helping you work smarter. But here's the thing: just because we *can* do something with AI doesn't always mean we *should*.

Like any powerful tool, AI comes with responsibilities. From protecting personal data to ensuring fair and ethical use, there are some very real challenges we need to navigate. In this chapter, I'll walk you through the potential privacy risks, the ethical responsibilities we all share when using AI, and some practical steps you can take to protect your data and use AI responsibly.

Privacy Risks in AI Tools

AI tools thrive on data. They learn, analyze, and improve based on the information we feed them. But this reliance on data also introduces privacy risks—especially when sensitive or personal information is involved.

1. Data Collection and Storage

Many AI tools require access to your data to function. For example:

- Language models like ChatGPT may temporarily store your inputs to improve performance.
- CRMs like Salesforce and HubSpot collect customer data to offer insights and predictions.

While this can be incredibly helpful, it also raises questions:

- Where is your data being stored?
- How long is it being kept?
- Who else has access to it?

The Risk: If data isn't properly encrypted or protected, it could be exposed in a breach, putting sensitive information at risk.

---

2. Third-Party Sharing

Some AI tools share user data with third parties, whether for analytics, advertising, or other purposes. This often happens behind the scenes, without you fully realizing it.

The Risk: Your data might end up in the hands of companies you don't know or trust, leading to unwanted targeted ads—or worse, malicious use.

---

3. Input Sensitivity

Here's one that doesn't always get talked about: the inputs you provide to AI tools. If you're using an AI tool to process sensitive information—like financial data, customer details, or even personal passwords—you might be inadvertently exposing that information.

The Risk: Depending on the tool's privacy policy, this data could be stored, analyzed, or even unintentionally leaked.

The Ethical Responsibility of Using AI

AI is an incredibly powerful tool—but with great power comes great responsibility (yes, I went there). As users, we have an ethical obligation to ensure that we're using AI tools in ways that are fair, transparent, and respectful of others' rights.

1. Avoiding Misuse of AI

AI isn't inherently good or bad—it all comes down to how we use it. Here are some common ways AI can be misused and why it's important to avoid them:

- **Manipulative Content:** Using AI to create deepfakes or misleading content that spreads false information.
- **Bias Amplification:** AI systems can unintentionally reflect and reinforce biases present in the data they're trained on. For example, a hiring tool might favor certain demographics if its training data is biased.
- **Surveillance and Privacy Violations:** Using AI to monitor people's behavior without their knowledge or consent.

Why It Matters: Misusing AI erodes trust and can have serious consequences, from harming individuals to damaging your reputation.

---

2. Transparency and Consent

When using AI tools that involve other people's data—whether it's customer information, employee records, or anything else—it's important to be transparent.

- Let people know when and how their data is being used.
- Always get consent before collecting or sharing sensitive information.

Why It Matters: Transparency builds trust, while secrecy or deception can lead to legal and ethical issues down the road.

---

3. Balancing Automation with Human Oversight

AI is amazing at automating tasks, but it's not perfect. Mistakes can happen, and it's up to us to catch them. For example:

- An AI tool might generate a biased recommendation or overlook important context.
- Automated processes might lead to errors if they're not reviewed by a human.

The Rule: AI should assist you—not replace your judgment or ethical considerations.

Practical Tips for Protecting Your Data

Now that we've talked about the risks and responsibilities, let's focus on how you can protect yourself and your data when using AI tools.

1. Read the Privacy Policy

I know, I know—privacy policies are boring. But they're also important. Look for answers to these questions:

- What data does the tool collect?
- How is your data stored and secured?
- Does the tool share your data with third parties?

Pro Tip: If the policy isn't clear or seems too invasive, it's a red flag.

---

2. Avoid Entering Sensitive Information

Be mindful of what you share with AI tools, especially if it's sensitive or confidential. For example:

- Don't input passwords, credit card numbers, or other private details into AI systems.
- Avoid using customer or client data unless you're sure it's secure.

Rule of Thumb: If you wouldn't share it publicly, don't share it with AI.

---

3. Use Trusted Tools

Stick to reputable AI platforms with strong security measures. Look for:

- Tools with end-to-end encryption.
- Companies that comply with data protection regulations like GDPR or CCPA.
- Tools with clear privacy policies and good reviews.

---

4. Regularly Audit Your AI Tools

Just like you'd check the apps on your phone or the software on your computer, take time to review the AI tools you're using:

- Are they still meeting your needs?
- Are they handling your data responsibly?
- Are there better, more secure alternatives available?

Why It Matters: Technology evolves quickly, and staying proactive ensures you're not left behind—or vulnerable.

---

5. Use Multi-Factor Authentication (MFA)

For tools that store sensitive data, enable multi-factor authentication to add an extra layer of security.

Why Ethics and Privacy Matter

AI has the power to transform the way we work, but it's up to us to use it responsibly. By understanding the risks, respecting ethical guidelines, and taking steps to protect your data, you're not just safeguarding yourself—you're contributing to a culture of trust and accountability around AI.

Here's the bottom line: AI is a tool, and like any tool, it can be used for good or bad. By staying informed and intentional about how you use AI, you can enjoy all its benefits without compromising on ethics or privacy.

In the final chapter, we'll explore how to plan your AI journey—setting goals, choosing tools, and building a long-term strategy for integrating AI into your work. Let's bring it all together!

Future Outlook and Action Plan

Chapter 13: Future Trends in AI for Productivity

Here's the thing about AI: it's constantly evolving. Just when you think you've got a handle on what it can do, a new breakthrough changes the game entirely. And while that can feel overwhelming, it's also incredibly exciting—especially when you think about how these advancements will shape the future of work and productivity.

In this chapter, we'll take a closer look at the AI trends that are already starting to emerge and how they're poised to revolutionize the way we work across industries. From generative AI to the integration of AI with the Internet of Things (IoT), let's dive into what the future holds.

Emerging AI Trends That Will Reshape the Workplace

1. Generative AI: Creating Beyond Limits

Generative AI has already started to make waves (just look at tools like ChatGPT and DALL·E), but it's just scratching the surface of what's possible. In the future, generative AI won't just assist with content creation—it'll redefine how we create, collaborate, and innovate.

- **Content Creation at Scale:** AI will be able to generate highly personalized content for marketing, training, and communication in real-time. Imagine AI crafting unique presentations, videos, or even e-learning courses tailored to specific audiences on the fly.
- **Design and Prototyping:** Architects, engineers, and product designers will use generative AI to create prototypes, test models, and simulate real-world conditions faster than ever before.
- **Creative Collaboration:** Generative AI will act as a creative partner, brainstorming new ideas, writing

first drafts, and even suggesting innovative solutions to complex problems.

Why It Matters: Generative AI isn't just about speeding up processes—it's about unlocking new levels of creativity and innovation.

---

2. The Convergence of AI and IoT

The Internet of Things (IoT) refers to all those "smart" devices—your smart fridge, smart thermostat, or even your smartwatch—that are connected to the internet and can communicate with each other. Now, imagine combining that with AI.

- **Smarter Workplaces:** AI-powered IoT devices will optimize office environments in real-time. For example, AI could adjust lighting, temperature, and even noise levels based on the time of day or the number of people in a room.
- **Seamless Automation:** In warehouses or manufacturing facilities, IoT devices equipped with AI will coordinate workflows, predict maintenance needs, and optimize supply chains without human intervention.
- **Enhanced Remote Work:** Smart home devices integrated with AI will create optimized remote work setups, automatically adjusting conditions to help you stay productive.

Why It Matters: AI and IoT together will create smarter, more efficient work environments that adapt to your needs without you even having to think about it.

---

3. AI-Powered Personal Assistants 2.0

We're already familiar with virtual assistants like Siri, Alexa, and Google Assistant. But the next generation of AI-powered assistants will take things to a whole new level.

- **Proactive Assistance:** Instead of waiting for you to give commands, these assistants will anticipate your needs. For example, they might remind you to follow up on an email based on your calendar or suggest a solution to a recurring problem at work.
- **Contextual Understanding:** AI assistants will get better at understanding context—like recognizing when you're in a meeting and automatically silencing notifications or summarizing key points from the discussion afterward.
- **Cross-Platform Integration:** Future AI assistants will seamlessly connect all your tools and platforms, making it feel like you have a personal productivity coach managing your workflow.

Why It Matters: These tools won't just save time; they'll help you work smarter by keeping you organized and proactive.

---

4. AI-Driven Decision-Making

As AI becomes more sophisticated, its ability to analyze data and make recommendations will become indispensable. In the future, we'll see AI-powered decision-making tools across every industry.

- **Scenario Modeling:** Businesses will use AI to simulate potential outcomes for decisions—like launching a new product or entering a new market—based on real-time data.
- **Risk Management:** AI will identify risks before they become problems, whether it's predicting cybersecurity threats or flagging operational inefficiencies.
- **Personalized Insights:** AI will provide tailored insights to individual employees, helping them make better decisions in their roles.

Why It Matters: AI won't just provide information—it'll give you the confidence to make data-driven decisions quickly and effectively.

The Impact of AI on Different Industries

The potential of AI goes far beyond individual productivity. Let's take a look at how it's set to transform some of the biggest industries out there.

1. Healthcare

- **Personalized Medicine:** AI will analyze genetic data and patient history to recommend highly personalized treatment plans.
- **Diagnostics:** AI tools will assist doctors in diagnosing diseases faster and with greater accuracy by analyzing medical images, lab results, and patient records.
- **Operational Efficiency:** Hospitals will use AI to optimize scheduling, manage inventory, and streamline patient care.

Example Impact: AI-powered tools could reduce diagnostic errors by up to 50%, saving lives and improving patient outcomes.

---

2. Education

- **Adaptive Learning:** AI will create customized learning experiences for students, adapting in real-time based on their progress and challenges.
- **Automated Grading:** Teachers will spend less time grading and more time focusing on instruction, thanks to AI systems that can evaluate assignments.
- **Virtual Classrooms:** AI will enhance online education with interactive, immersive experiences that mimic in-person learning.

Example Impact: Students in remote areas will gain access to high-quality education tailored to their individual needs.

---

3. Retail

- **Customer Personalization:** AI will recommend products based on individual shopping habits, making every customer's experience unique.
- **Inventory Management:** Retailers will use AI to predict demand and optimize stock levels, reducing waste and maximizing profits.
- **Automated Checkout:** AI-powered checkout systems will eliminate the need for long lines, creating a smoother shopping experience.

Example Impact: Businesses will see increased sales and customer loyalty through hyper-personalized shopping experiences.

---

4. Finance

- **Fraud Detection:** AI will analyze transactions in real time to detect and prevent fraudulent activity.
- **Financial Planning:** Banks and financial advisors will use AI to offer personalized investment and savings recommendations.
- **Automation:** From loan approvals to tax filing, AI will handle routine financial processes with speed and accuracy.

Example Impact: Consumers will enjoy faster services, while businesses save millions through reduced fraud and operational costs.

Why These Trends Matter

AI is no longer just a tool—it's becoming an integral part of how we work, live, and solve problems. The trends we've explored here aren't just exciting—they're transformative. They'll reshape industries, create new opportunities, and challenge us to think differently about what's possible.

But here's the kicker: the future of AI isn't just about the technology itself. It's about how we choose to use it. Will we use it to make work more meaningful and lives more fulfilling? Or will we let it replace the very human connections that drive us? That choice is ours to make.

As we look ahead, one thing is clear: AI's potential is limitless. Whether you're an entrepreneur, an employee, or a leader, understanding and embracing these trends will give you a front-row seat to the future of productivity.

In the next and final chapter, we'll explore how you can create your personalized action plan to integrate AI into your work and life. Let's wrap this journey up strong!

Chapter 14: Creating Your AI Action Plan

By now, you've learned all about the incredible ways AI can transform your productivity, streamline your workflows, and even spark your creativity. But here's the thing: none of it matters unless you take action. The tools and strategies we've covered are only as effective as your willingness to implement them in your daily life. That's where an action plan comes in.

In this final chapter, I'll guide you through creating a personalized AI application plan that fits your unique needs. Whether you're an entrepreneur, a freelancer, or part of a larger organization, you'll learn how to identify the best tools, set goals, and continuously optimize your approach. Let's turn everything we've talked about into a roadmap for success.

How to Create a Personalized AI Application Plan

Let's start with the basics: what exactly is an AI application plan? Think of it as your blueprint for integrating AI into your work and life. It's not about overwhelming yourself with every tool under the sun—it's about identifying your goals, starting small, and building from there.

Step 1: Identify Your Pain Points

Before you can decide which AI tools to use, you need to figure out where they can make the biggest impact. Ask yourself:

- What tasks or processes take up most of my time?
- Where am I struggling to stay organized or efficient?
- What areas of my work could benefit from automation or better insights?

Example Pain Points:

- Spending hours writing emails or reports.
- Manually organizing data or creating charts.
- Struggling to keep track of deadlines and projects.
- Needing fresh ideas for content or marketing.

Step 2: Set Clear Goals

Once you've identified your pain points, set specific goals for how AI can help. These should be measurable and tied to real outcomes.

Examples of AI Goals:

- Save 5 hours a week by automating repetitive tasks.
- Increase blog output from 1 post per week to 3 using AI writing tools.
- Improve customer response times by integrating an AI chatbot.

- Reduce time spent on data analysis by 50% with tools like Tableau or Power BI.

Step 3: Choose the Right Tools

Now that you know what you want to achieve, it's time to pick the AI tools that align with your goals. Here's a quick cheat sheet to help:

Goal	Recommended Tools
Automate repetitive tasks	Zapier, Automate.io, Calendly
Write content faster	ChatGPT, Jasper, Grammarly
Create visuals or designs	Canva, DALL·E
Analyze data and trends	Power BI, Tableau, Google Data Studio
Manage customer relationships	Salesforce AI (Einstein), HubSpot, Zoho CRM
Improve time management	Motion, Notion AI, RescueTime

Pro Tip: Start with one or two tools, and don't worry about getting everything perfect right away. The goal is progress, not perfection.

Step 4: Test and Iterate

Once you've chosen your tools, it's time to put them to work. Here's how to approach the testing phase:

- **Start Small:** Automate a single task or use an AI tool for one project.
- **Measure Results:** Track how much time you save, how your output improves, or how your stress levels change.
- **Refine Your Approach:** If something isn't working, tweak your process or try a different tool.

Example: Let's say you're using ChatGPT to draft blog posts. After a few weeks, you realize the AI's tone doesn't always match your brand voice. You adjust your prompts to be more specific about tone and style, and suddenly the results improve dramatically.

A Simple AI Integration Template to Get Started

Here's a quick template you can use to create your personalized AI action plan:

1. Identify Your Goals:

- Example: "I want to reduce the time I spend on writing reports by 50%."

2. Choose Your Tools:

- Example: ChatGPT for drafting reports, Grammarly for polishing language.

3. Define Your Workflow:

- Example: "Use ChatGPT to generate a first draft based on key points, then edit and finalize using Grammarly."

4. Set Metrics for Success:

- Example: "Complete reports in 2 hours instead of 4, without compromising quality."

5. Review and Optimize:

- Example: "After two weeks, assess whether the process is saving time and adjust prompts or tools if needed."

Next Steps: How to Keep Improving Your AI Skills

Integrating AI isn't a one-and-done deal. As tools evolve and your needs change, it's important to keep learning and optimizing your approach. Here's how:

1. Stay Curious

AI is constantly evolving, with new tools and features being released all the time. Make it a habit to:

- Explore updates to your existing tools.
- Experiment with new tools that align with your goals.
- Follow industry blogs or newsletters to stay informed.

---

2. Learn from Others

You don't have to figure everything out on your own. Join communities where other professionals share tips, strategies, and success stories about using AI.

- Check out forums like Reddit's r/artificial or LinkedIn groups for AI professionals.
- Watch YouTube tutorials or attend webinars for hands-on demonstrations.

---

3. Regularly Audit Your AI Workflow

Every few months, take a step back and evaluate:

- Are your current tools still meeting your needs?
- Are there new features or integrations you haven't tried yet?
- Are there tasks you're still doing manually that could be automated?

Pro Tip: Keep a list of recurring tasks that frustrate you. As new AI tools emerge, revisit that list to see if there's a solution available.

Why This Action Plan Matters

Here's the truth: AI isn't just a passing trend. It's a tool that's here to stay—and it's only going to get better. The people who thrive in this new era of work will be the ones who know how to use AI effectively, ethically, and strategically.

By creating a personalized AI action plan, you're not just learning how to use a few tools—you're building a foundation for long-term success. Whether your goal is to save time, grow your business, or simply make work a little easier, the steps you take today will set you up for a more productive, less stressful tomorrow.

So here's my challenge to you: don't wait. Start small, experiment, and make AI a part of your workflow today. You've got all the knowledge you need—now it's time to put it into action.

Thank you for joining me on this journey. Here's to a future where you work smarter, achieve more, and enjoy the process along the way. Let's go make it happen!

Appendix: Your AI Productivity Toolkit

So, you've made it through the book and you're ready to dive into the world of AI. But where do you start? Don't worry—I've got you covered. This appendix is your go-to resource for tools, learning materials, and practical templates to help you hit the ground running. Think of it as your AI productivity starter pack.

Recommended AI Tools and Their Uses

Here's a curated list of AI tools, organized by category, to help you choose the right ones for your needs. I've included links so you can check them out directly.

1. Content Creation

- **ChatGPT (OpenAI)**
    - **Use:** Writing blog posts, social media captions, emails, and brainstorming ideas.
    - **Website:** https://chat.openai.com
- **Jasper**

- **Use:** Marketing copy, ads, and SEO-optimized content.
    - **Website:** https://www.jasper.ai
- **Canva**
    - **Use:** Designing graphics, presentations, and documents with AI-powered suggestions.
    - **Website:** https://www.canva.com
- **DALL·E (OpenAI)**
    - **Use:** Generating custom images from text prompts.
    - **Website:** https://openai.com/dall-e

2. Task Automation

- **Zapier**
    - **Use:** Automating workflows between apps like Gmail, Slack, and Google Sheets.
    - **Website:** https://zapier.com
- **Automate.io**
    - **Use:** Streamlining repetitive tasks across platforms.
    - **Website:** https://automate.io
- **Calendly**
    - **Use:** Automating meeting scheduling.
    - **Website:** https://calendly.com

3. Data Analysis

- **Power BI (Microsoft)**
    - **Use:** Creating data visualizations and reports.

- **Website:** https://powerbi.microsoft.com
- **Tableau**
  - **Use:** Interactive dashboards and data analysis.
  - **Website:** https://www.tableau.com
- **Google Data Studio**
  - **Use:** Free tool for creating custom dashboards and reports.
  - **Website:** https://datastudio.google.com

4. Customer Relationship Management (CRM)

- **Salesforce Einstein**
  - **Use:** AI-driven CRM for lead scoring, customer insights, and workflow automation.
  - **Website:** https://www.salesforce.com
- **HubSpot CRM**
  - **Use:** Managing customer relationships and automating marketing campaigns.
  - **Website:** https://www.hubspot.com
- **Zoho CRM**
  - **Use:** AI assistant for customer management and actionable insights.
  - **Website:** https://www.zoho.com/crm

5. Productivity and Time Management

- **Notion AI**
  - **Use:** Organizing tasks, projects, and notes with AI-powered assistance.
  - **Website:** https://www.notion.so

- **Motion**
    - **Use:** Combining scheduling and task management with AI suggestions.
    - **Website:** https://www.usemotion.com
- **RescueTime**
    - **Use:** Tracking time usage and improving productivity.
    - **Website:** https://www.rescuetime.com

AI Learning Resources: Websites, Courses, and Communities

If you want to deepen your understanding of AI and stay ahead of the curve, here are some great places to learn and connect with like-minded individuals.

1. Websites and Blogs

- **Towards Data Science**
    - Blog covering AI trends, tutorials, and case studies.
    - https://towardsdatascience.com
- **OpenAI Blog**
    - Updates and insights from the creators of ChatGPT and DALL·E.
    - https://openai.com/blog
- **AI for Everyone by Andrew Ng (Coursera)**
    - Beginner-friendly course on AI's impact and applications.

- https://www.coursera.org/learn/ai-for-everyone

2. Online Courses

- **Elements of AI**
  - Free course designed to teach the basics of AI.
  - https://www.elementsofai.com
- **Fast.ai**
  - Hands-on courses for learning machine learning and AI applications.
  - https://www.fast.ai
- **Udemy AI Courses**
  - Affordable courses on topics like AI for business, machine learning, and more.
  - https://www.udemy.com

3. Communities and Forums

- **Reddit (r/artificial)**
  - A community for discussing AI trends, tools, and innovations.
  - https://www.reddit.com/r/artificial
- **LinkedIn Groups**
  - Search for AI-related groups like "AI Enthusiasts" or "AI for Business" to connect with professionals.
- **Kaggle**
  - A platform for AI and data science competitions and discussions.

- https://www.kaggle.com

Practical Prompt Templates for AI Tools

To help you get started with AI tools, here's a collection of practical prompt templates you can customize for your needs.

1. Writing Content

- **Blog Post Draft:**
  "Write a 500-word blog post about [topic]. Use a friendly tone, include 3 key points, and end with a call-to-action."
- **Social Media Caption:**
  "Create a catchy Instagram caption for [product/service]. Include a hashtag and a call-to-action to visit the website."

2. Task Automation

- **Email Follow-Up Reminder:**
  "Set a reminder to follow up with [client name] three days after our initial email."
- **Data Sync Automation:**
  "When a new row is added to Google Sheets, send a Slack notification to [team channel]."

3. Data Analysis

- **Sales Trends Summary:**
  "Analyze this sales data and summarize the top 3 trends. Include any notable anomalies and recommendations for next month."
- **Dashboard Request:**
  "Create a dashboard that tracks [specific metrics] over time. Use a bar chart for [metric A] and a line graph for [metric B]."

4. Customer Engagement

- **Customer Email Draft:**
  "Write a professional email to a customer apologizing for a delay in delivery. Be empathetic and offer a discount code as compensation."
- **Chatbot Script:**
  "Draft a chatbot conversation for answering FAQs about [product/service]. Include responses for questions about pricing, shipping, and returns."

Final Thoughts

This appendix is your toolkit to start exploring AI with confidence. Whether you're just dipping your toes into automation or ready to integrate AI into every corner of your work, these resources, tools, and templates will help you get there faster.

Remember, the key to mastering AI is to keep experimenting, learning, and refining your approach. You don't need to know everything to get started—you just need to take the first step. The future of productivity is here, and you're ready to be part of it.

Good luck, and here's to your AI-powered journey!

Note

This book is a culmination of my personal experiences, daily practices, and hands-on interactions with various AI tools. It reflects the knowledge I've gained through exploring how AI can enhance productivity and solve real-world problems.

Additionally, I've leveraged the capabilities of AI itself to enrich this book. From generating insights to organizing content, AI has been both a tool and a collaborator in the process. By combining my practical knowledge with the support of AI-generated suggestions, I've aimed to create a comprehensive guide that is both accessible and actionable for readers.

My hope is that this book not only informs but also inspires you to embrace AI and discover the countless ways it can transform the way you work and live.